For Lisa, Joel, Luke and Ashley – you have all my love.

Foreword

When Phil Shelton asked me to write a Foreword for his book, I wasn't sure what to expect (from the book). After all, there are myriad books about how to succeed in various careers, including high-tech careers.

But the more I looked around, the more I realized that most of those books are for people starting or moving through management positions of some type or another. There really are very few books available for entry-level workforce people. And fewer still are as easy to read and entertaining as this one!

What Phil Shelton has done is consolidate decades of experience into a series of lessons and anecdotes that entertain, teach, and reinforce best practices in the workplace. I read this entire book in one sitting, which I rarely do with any book. Within these pages, Phil provides sage advice, shares entertaining missteps, and passes on the wisdom that often comes only with perspective.

At Oregon Tech, we commonly tell our students that they may get their first job with their skills and knowledge of a topic, but they will succeed in that job (or not) based on a whole host of other criteria. Phil Shelton has done a remarkable job of outlining those other criteria (reputation, relationships, work ethic, life balance, lifelong learning, integrity, communication, reactions, and many others) in a way that is both entertaining and memorable.

So who should read this book and why? Frankly, I believe that anyone in the working world would benefit from reading Phil's book. But for those who are about to embark on your first career move (and don't forget, this often may be your first internship or externship!), this book should be required reading.

Although the modern workforce track is not one that likely will see you make a career with a single company, you will find outstanding and relevant advice, guidance, and lessons within these pages. Everything, from the Golden Rule to focusing on non-monetary enrichment (monetary enrichment usually follows happy, successful people), is contained within these pages.

Phil Shelton has done us a favor by being a mentor from a distance with his book. Even as a university president, I found myself learning and reminiscing about my own mistakes, many of which I may have avoided if Phil's book had been available several years ago.

Enjoy the book. Read all or parts of it in almost any order. Put it where you can see it and reread parts every now and again, as you advance in your career. I believe you'll find the wisdom contained in these words to be excellent periodic course checks that will keep you on track towards your own life goals.

Christopher G. Maples, President
Oregon Institute of Technology

Prologue

This is a manual for college juniors and seniors about to start their career in the corporate world, either as an intern or a full-time employee. It's geared towards technical students with degrees such as computer science or engineering, but the principles in this book could apply to anyone's career.

Parker/Banks Publishing
Orange County, CA

Thanks to everyone who helped make this book possible especially Guy Ball, Mark Dickinson and John Rose.

How to read this book

Some of the things you read in here will rise to the level of "nuggets of wisdom." Not because I said them, but because they are the gleaned from years of people's crash and burn experiences (including mine!) and more importantly from our successes. You're reaping the benefits of many significant career lessons without having to sit down and interview a bunch of people who have been there and done that. I marked these words of wisdom with an attention icon to get you to pause and think about them for a bit without skipping right over them.

Congratulations

So you're sitting there with a head full of book knowledge and hopefully a few mad technical skills, ready to embark on a career that will define your life... This is a big step for you personally and professionally (yes, you will have a "professional" status now). This is a moment that you have prepared for with 72% or so of your life - 16 years, give or take that fifth year in college. This is something you want to get right.

The best way to determine what your career will look like is to plan, ahead of time, how you present yourself. The decisions you make right now on what your character, attitude and work ethic will be - these will determine how your career goes much more than any event that happens to you at the company who hires you.

To help you decide what kind of person you want to be known as in your career, I'll talk about some major pitfalls to avoid and some things that successful people consistently do. Your ability to use these lessons to gain perspective on your career and make smart choices will help determine whether you will be more like Dilbert or Billbert (Bill Gates) on the scale of career success.

The first and most important attribute of your career will be your reputation. Your first few days and weeks on the job will determine whether coworkers and management think of you as someone who is punctual, hard-working and dependable with a good attitude or whether you get the infamous "but" attached to you. "Yeah, he's nice and has good potential, but he's not serious about succeeding here since he's not always on time." Or "Yeah, she's got great skills but she's always complaining or pointing out why something is difficult to do."

Your reputation is something to be tended and nurtured. It will determine whether you get put on the most important projects or assigned to the generic "people pool" that gets allocated to whatever comes along.

So the big picture here at the start of your career is that there are two "R's" (Relationships and Reputation) which are critical to your success. These will have more to do with your success, at least at the start of your career, than your hard-earned technical skills. Let's discuss how to get started building these from Day One on the job and then figure out how to grow your technical skills.

Building Your Reputation

There's no substitute for hard work. Show up on time, every time. If you're work starts at 8:00, get there at 7:45 so you can get your coffee and be at your desk ready for business on time. Rolling in the parking lot at 8:00 gets you on the B-team, which later becomes the X-team (as in EX-employee once the economic downturn and layoff cycles start). Same thing for leaving early, don't do it! Your work group will have a certain culture. If the culture of that group is 8 to 5, you'll be throwing away reputational currency if you leave at 4:30 every day. For this reason, I suggest that people to live close to where they work if at all possible - for at least the first part of your career. You want to be the one who can come in early and stay late when needed. This is the "paying your dues" part of your career – getting started, coming to a new company and establishing your reputation. Its hard work but it won't last that long. You will also learn who the "serious workers" are at your company, people you can trust to get things done and do a good job instead of just punching the clock.

Surviving Crunch Time

There will be times at work that are critical: finishing up an important project that your biggest customer has been counting on, delivering a flagship product on time, or finishing a proposal by the bid deadline. These are the 60 hour weeks and the weekends with no social life. This is the time to earn your credibility and achieve something that stays with you for many years. These times will pass and they are short, get in there and work hard with a ridiculously good attitude. Be a positive attitude on that stressed out team, for you may be their leader one day.

Professionalism

One of the most important factors in determining what your reputation will be is your professionalism. What is professionalism? It's answering every e-mail or phone call you get, even if it's to say you're not the right one to handle that question or problem but here's someone who is - and give them a name. It's putting your Out Of Office (OoO) notification on when you're gone for a vacation day or you have to take off the afternoon to go to the doctor. If you deal with customers on the phone, it's recording an OoO voice mail telling them when you'll return and who to talk to while you're out if there's something urgent. It's calling in sick before starting time in the morning to let your manager or the secretary know you're going to be out.

Professionalism is being where you say you're going to be, every time every day. In the rare circumstances where something happens to prevent this, it's letting everyone who counts on you know what's going on. For some of you, this type of life structure will come naturally. But for others it will have to be a learned skill. If you don't learn it fast, you'll hear about it at your first performance review...

Protecting Your Reputation

It's important to realize that one moment of levity or anger can damage your reputation, sometimes beyond repair in that group or at that company. The workplace is not a college campus. One off-the-cuff sexist or racist joke at a work party or a derogatory comment about someone at the water cooler can blow serious holes in your reputation. Reputations take a long time to build but can be destroyed in a moment. You're a professional now, don't go there. Stay out of the proverbial gutter. You'll work with people who always seem to be out there on the fringe of acceptability, but if you don't ever go there you won't have to dig yourself out or deal with the consequences.

Staying away from angry emotional comments and the wrong kind of humor is not only true for your direct relationships with the people you see every day - it's even more important for those you deal with via e-mail. What you type and send over the internet can stay around forever. If it's bad, a written copy of it is likely to show up in the hands of your boss when you least expect and want it. Never, never, never write and send a scathing reply to something you just read. That moment of emotion will look so out of place and out of character when you read it a month from now, and it will get you in trouble. You will see people who can't seem to resist doing this, but it's like shooting at someone with a gun that has a plugged barrel that could blow up in your face. Take a walk, cool down, and get some perspective. Even if your anger is righteous (i.e. someone blamed you for something that wasn't your fault) there's a business-professional way to frame your answer. State the facts, document how this situation occurred (if necessary) and provide a recommendation to fix it.

Whatever, you do, make sure the situation does get resolved. Never let bad situations fester or they will become chronically infected like an untreated wound (I know this is an ugly word picture but actually it's nothing compared to the daily pain of an unresolved conflict with a co-worker).

In addition to not doing the wrong things, there are a lot of right things you can do to protect and grow your reputation. Your reputation grows when you're unselfish. Look for opportunities to learn things outside the scope of your current job and don't have blinders on regarding what your job description is. When you look for ways to improve the productivity of your group or your company you'll be more than just another employee - you'll be a leader. Think of people like Steve Wozniak, Michael Dell or Steve Jobs or anyone else who rose to significant corporate leadership. These people didn't color inside the lines defined by their predecessors.

To grow into a position of leadership you will need the ability to make sound decisions with less than perfect information. You will rarely have all the information it would take to make a riskless decision, so you'll have to take the best information you have and fill in the gaps with knowledge, experience and counsel. In these cases, make your decision logical and defendable. This should be your normal MO 99% of the time - logical and defendable. Just keep your eye out for that rare 1% occasion, where making a not so logical leap of faith to roll the dice based on a huge potential business upside could be a career or company game changer. For example, my company had the chance to be the first Fibre Channel Storage Area Network (SAN) enclosure supplier to a startup company with visions of grandeur. Our division VP at the time made a logical and defendable decision not to provide that company with a large quantity of expensive storage subsystems they had requested as free samples. However, as a result, the relationship never got started and the company went elsewhere for their storage. The scope of this missed opportunity turned out to be drastic - we could've got in on the ground floor with NetApp…

Building Relationships

Everyone you meet at work has the potential to be someone you work with or for in the future. They could even end up working for you someday. So don't make any enemies by saying stupid things to or about your co-workers. How you treat the jerks can be just as important as how you treat your friends. Whether you respect their opinion (even if you don't agree with it) will determine how accepted and successful you are as their manager one day. There's always something you can learn from everyone, even if it's a lesson in reverse - how not to do something.

There are going to be a few key relationships at work that are important and worth investing in. Discussions and time spent with these people are not just good business, they are an investment in a life well lived. We spend a significant portion of our lives at work, so these high quality friends can make a huge positive impact in your life. However, picking friends at work is just like picking friends at school - you need to pick friends who are good people who want to succeed and inspire you to greater things, not friends who drag you down into mediocrity and apathy.

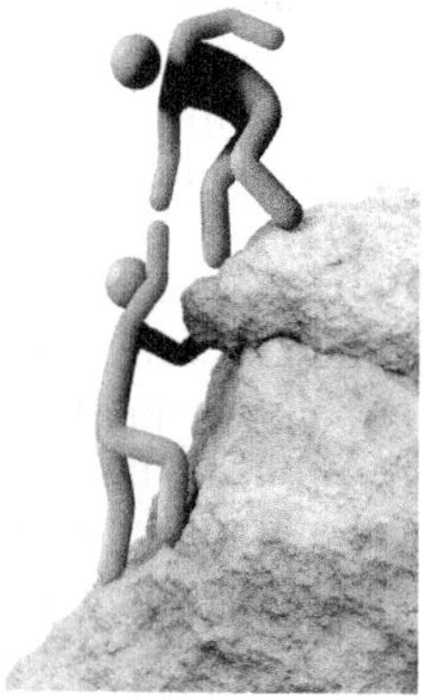

Work friends who inspire and encourage you can become long term or even lifetime friends. They will stay important even if your career paths diverge (i.e. one of you ends up at a different company). They will also be the first ones you will turn to in the event things go south where you're at now and you're looking for new opportunities.

If you work hard and have good relationships, then what you think is the biggest goal of your career (making money) will take care of itself. Your career focus needs to be about more than just "all about the Benjamin's." There's nothing wrong with having an internal motivation to succeed so you can reap the financial rewards of your hard work, that's admirable ambition. But you won't be happy unless you have the internal satisfaction of doing a good job and the feeling of social support you get when you're connected with your co-workers. And while being happy may not sound like an important career goal, your career will not be fulfilling and sustainable unless you take your happiness into account along the way.

We tend to think that when we make X amount of money or have Y amount of possessions or get a house we'll be happy. Take it from those of us who are down the road a ways, the time to be happy is while you're on the journey - not at the end of it. Not only that, but what you will find is that your end of the journey target (your success goal of X-money or Y-possessions) keeps moving once you achieve the first goal. Even if you're one of those rare people who can put a cap on your materialistic goals so that you're reasonably content once you achieve your first financial goal, it will be a hollow victory unless you have someone to share it with.

There's one other thing you need to realize on the journey towards success - there's nothing wrong or deficient with you early in your career if don't have enough money to support yourself or your family the way you would like to. It's just the stage of life you're in - it's normal and respectable. It's ironic; at the start of your career it will feel like you work the hardest and get paid the least. Then later in your career you make bigger bucks for less physical work but more strategic decision making and leadership, while a fresh group of college graduates are paying their dues and working up to where you are.

Relationships with difficult people - yes, you will have them. Like perfectionist co-workers who can't understand people who don't know everything they do. Or self serving managers (otherwise known as "PHB's" - Pointy Haired Bosses from Dilbert) who pursue short term goals and bonuses at the expense of the complete truth - whose success is often the result of the outstanding work you performed. Look on the bright side. It's been my experience that a hard working person with integrity will outlast the PHBs.

There will be co-workers that have a chip on their shoulder and don't like anyone, or they may even decide they have a particular grudge against you. Then there will always be a certain percentage of people that don't like you, for no good reason. You can't make everyone happy and you shouldn't try to - the goal of having great relationships at work is achievable, but almost never with all of the people all the time.

There's another relationship that you need to pay special attention to. This won't take a lot of time, but there's a big down side if you don't invest anything in this relationship. Of course I'm talking about the office secretary, administrative assistant or office manager. She (or he) gets paid a lot less than you do for the privilege of dealing with all of you relationship-challenged technical geeks and prima donna managers. Take some time to chat with this person and learn how they see the world of this workplace. That will be a reality check on whether you're in touch with who the important people are in this part of the company and how they are viewed. Make sure you treat this person well. Graciously thank them when they help you and help them in return when you can. You don't want to be on their bad side - they can make your life miserable. On the other hand, having a good relationship with the person who handles the office supplies is a big plus when you need something. ☺

A final note on how to handle relationships with integrity – accept the fact ahead of time that you will make mistakes. This is normal and when you look back at the mistakes you made later with some perspective, you'll realize these were the times you learned the most. The important thing to know about mistakes on the job is that the consequences of them are minimal and they go away quickly when you admit you made them, say "I'm sorry" and "I learned from it." The moment you do that, the problem is old news and the page is turned. However, if you attempt to hide or bury the mistake it will eventually come back to haunt you. Your reputation and trust will take a hit with the team - and people will be less willing to admit their mistakes to you (which is a killer if you plan on ever being their manager). You have to prove you can handle mistakes humbly and move on from them with a good attitude. This will allow you to accept other's mistakes as well, which is a key factor in good team relationships.

As bad as fleeing the scene of a mistake without making things right is, there's one thing that's worse – looking for someone else to blame. If only they had done this (whatever it is) I wouldn't have been in that situation. If they hadn't done that (whatever it is) I wouldn't have blah blah blah… Remember this, to blame is to BLame (Be Lame). You wouldn't want someone else blaming you for their mistake, so man up, tell the truth and get past it.

How I got started

When I was sitting where you are, as a senior in college getting ready to graduate, I made two of the most important decisions in my career – before I even interviewed for a single job or knew what kind of boss I would work for! I made them because that's the way I wanted to live and who I wanted to be, but I thought these "how I'm going to act" decisions were pretty irrelevant to my career success. I couldn't have been more wrong. But it turned out that I was wrong in a good way. I decided that I would do business with absolute integrity (the honesty policy) and be nice to everybody (the golden rule). Little did I know that the moment the concrete of those ideas hardened in my will that my career was already on track to be successful. Doing these two things will put you ahead of 75% of the people you work with, people who will be going for the same promotions and raises as you.

Being nice to everyone

What you will discover is that getting mad at people and blasting them with angry words (even if they deserve it) can have dire consequences. Take the high road! You will disagree with people, but there is a right way to handle it. You can argue about the actions to take or the results of a failed strategy, but never attack someone's character or motives. When you do this, you're creating an enemy and burning a bridge that you may need later. By the way, this is a great lesson for when you get married. Arguments are ok, but going beyond the scope of what you're arguing about and saying character-damaging things like "you're a jerk/loser/etc." or "you always..." is poison to a relationship. In your life and career, it's all about the relationships! This may be a new concept for an engineer who plans to make their living with technical skills, but the opportunities for you to apply those technical skills on important projects will depend on the quality of your relationships and your ability to communicate them to others.

Doing business with integrity

The most important part of having integrity at work is keeping your word. When you tell someone you'll do something for them or have an answer to their question by a certain date you have to make it happen. So you better tell them a realistic date in the first place. Resist the temptation to make people happy by giving them a best case if-I-spend-all-my-time-on-this answer. If you ever, ever, ever have to miss a commitment (i.e. to higher priority things coming up) and I mean to anyone! even some low level person in a department far far away who you think could never have any impact on your career - you must always call or e-mail them. Tell them what happened and that you will be late then provide a new date for meeting your commitment. You should have a mental self-induced taser that threatens to go off when you are in danger of letting a written or spoken commitment go by without meeting it or telling the person you will be late.

You'll see that the people compromise their integrity by doing things like fudging schedules to look good or exaggerating their accomplishments. Making a good noise to the boss may put off a confrontation with truth for a week or two, but the truth will always catch up to you - bringing a load of embarrassment and a loss of credibility. Once you establish a reputation as a straight shooter who tells the truth (even if it's not good news) guess who the VP will come to next time they need an honest opinion on the status of a critical project? One note about telling the truth on schedules and cost: sometimes an over-zealous line manager who cares about staying out of the critical path more than the truth will "encourage" you to present an unrealistic schedule. If this happens, you can defer trouble by making a schedule diagram with a best case date (what the boss wants) and a realistic date (the real schedule). Provide them both and then make sure you save the e-mail you sent them in, so whenever this project goes into the "Search for the Guilty" phase[1] you're covered. You will outlast managers like this.

[1] http://en.wikipedia.org/wiki/Six_phases_of_a_big_project

Another way in which people are usually tempted to compromise their integrity is downplay problems that occurred in product testing (or in other words "tell the boss what they want to hear"). Of course the boss doesn't want to hear there was a failure during system test which could delay the first customer ship of an important product. Especially if the problem only happened once and it hasn't happened again, the temptation would be to confirm it's reproducible before telling anyone and think if it never happens again it wasn't a real problem. Wrong answer! My experience has been that this phantom problem will show up in the field, usually at your first customer! Integrity means you tell the truth, track the problem and all the attempts to reproduce it and have the whole team make a decision on whether to ship or not. This makes it a shared responsibility situation (a good thing), not your fault alone (a bad thing).

Being nice to everyone whether they deserve it or not, and doing business with integrity no matter what the circumstance. These are the pillars I built my reputation on.

So now you know the two character goals I started my career with. What will be yours? You will be known for something, so it's better to choose what you want to be known as - then start doing things that make yourself known as that person!

Stories

There are times when things are so bad you just have to laugh about them.

There was one occasion when my company took over a contract to provide a special I/O module which connected disk and tape drives to a mainframe computer system. The contract was already two months late when we started working on it. By the time we got prototype hardware installed at the customer site in a brand new building, the site was in production and attaching hardware to the production system could only be done in off-hours (12 midnight to 6:00am). After a few nights of this, everything was installed and running like a top. I remember sleeping all the way home on the long flight. Early the next day, the site called and said a lightning strike the previous night had fried all the disks we just installed! (Since the building was new, the site didn't have surge protection installed yet). And oh yeah, could I be there the next day to get the cleanup started and make sure everything was ready for a reinstall with new hardware ASAP? Wow. So back out I went, saying hello the same flight crew and stewardesses from two days before.

After a week on site, the surge protection was installed and the new disks (external disk drives the size of a washing machine) were up and running in production about 3:00 in the morning. Just as I closed the door to the data center and thought "it's finally done" there was a big explosion in the datacenter! "Come on, no way! That's just wrong!" I thought. But when I went back in the datacenter I was shocked - everything was still running. There was a haze in the air, so I started to investigate. One of the halon (fire extinguisher) canisters under the floor had exploded, leaving a missing floor tile on the raised floor as evidence. I looked around for the floor tile, trying to figure out where it blew away to. Finally I looked up and the floor tile was stuck in the ceiling! Yikes, if I had been standing on top of that tile I could have been killed. Luckily this customer was pretty much stable after the reinstall and I didn't ever have to go back there.

Tough people last, tough situations don't.

Avoid the game changing turnovers.

One of the friends I made along the way was a software genius named Bob Carter from Pennsylvania. We went as a team to do a few customer installs and our relationship was one of those great combinations of professionalism and constant humor. I was installing systems at a site where Bob was supposed to show up a couple of days later, after the job he was working on was completed. When he showed up two days early I was surprised and asked him what happened. He got a sheepish look and said "I was kicked out of the NSA and banned for life". "What?!" I said, "What happened?" He explained that he was installing a new group of disk drives at the NSA, and that he had a test program to perform read/write testing on the new disks - to make sure they worked before turning them over to the customer. Well, his test program had a bug and didn't just write to the new bank of disk drives - it overwrote every one of the 200+ disk drives in the NSA data center! To make matters worse, the test data pattern his program wrote on the disks was his name "BobCarterBobCarterBobCarter..." - as if there were any doubt who had done it (insert a big Homer Simpson "D'oh!" here). It took the site over a day to recover all the data from their backup tapes.

Talk about a big time booboo, wow.

Building your Technical skills

If you're like most people, some portion of the specific technical skills you learned in college will be different from the ones required on your first job. That's nothing to be concerned about. Every company that hires a new college graduate expects to spend time training that person with the specific skills they require. One of the most important things you learned in college was how-to-learn (a technical skill or anything). For example, your ability to learn that first programming language makes learning the next one an incremental effort, not a start from scratch scenario.

Hopefully one of the other things you picked up along the way is an effective system for learning. The better type of system you have for documenting things you learn and prioritizing them into a logical pattern in your memory, the better you will be at learning any technical or business skill on your job. I suggest keeping a notebook or computer file which contains every scrap of important information you learn along the way, like a job journal. I had one for every significant project I worked on through the years. This will give you a handy reference for things like procedures, reference diagrams and even contacts. At the end of each week, try to set aside a few minutes to enter any important contacts you made that week as vcards in Exchange or whatever mail application you use.

One of the best, fastest and easiest ways to build your technical expertise at a company is to get a mentor. If your company doesn't automatically match you up with a senior engineer to mentor you, go look for one. You want to learn from someone who knows a lot about what you will have the potential to do in a year or five years - someone who is preferably the go-to technical person for that department or facility. The most ideal situation is a mentor that works as a senior to you on the project you're assigned to.

That way you get a chance to observe them, learn their technical skills and problem solving methodology. Basically you want to drain their brain of any knowledge you will need to succeed, so that you become their technical equivalent plus all of your other skills and good attitude. You may not ever make it to the point of being as completely technically knowledgeable as them since your relationship may not span years, but it's a good goal to start with. One of the possible career options that may come your way is that you could be called upon to replace your mentor in the event they retire or move to another company (which is pretty common in this industry, especially for people with significant technical skills).

One of the side benefits of having a mentor is that you will have a person who models for you how to successfully fit in to the culture of that company. Even if your mentor turns out to be an anti-social nerd who rarely ever leaves the engineering lab, they can provide lessons in how not to fit into the culture. Sometimes a negative example is just as easy to learn from as a positive one.

My first technical mentor was an EE graduate who designed the circuit boards and did low level assembly programming on the I/O interface boards that got installed in mainframe computers and allowed them to talk to external disk and tape drives. Bill was a 6'4" big fella who looked just about like Chewbacca the Wookie from Star Wars. He was definitely in the latter category for socially fitting into the company culture (an anti-social technical wizard). But he could solve any hardware problem with his analyzer expertise or find the cause of a software bug by tracing code or viewing signals on an oscilloscope. Whenever management needed a "no BS" technical update or schedule outlook, Bill (whose initials are ironically BS) was the go-to guy. I learned a methodical problem solving technique from Bill - things like change one variable at a time then retest and document everything.

I also learned the patience of waiting until all the technical facts are in and analyzed before providing an "it's fixed" update to management. And that providing status on the resolution of a critical problem is best done when there's significant progress to report. Keeping management in the loop every half an hour gets messy when there's a half a day delay due to the tools not working or you're in the "hmm, this looks wrong, how does this product ever work?" stage of tracing how the hardware and code work together (after you've been through a few problem debugs you'll know what I mean). You don't want management going off and making decisions based on this meaningless interim status, which will soon be superseded by real progress.

The best way to grow your technical skills is to never stop learning. This will be true in every stage of your career. Whenever you're not in a critical project phase that's taking every working hour, seek out and volunteer for every class, seminar and learning opportunity that's related to your job. After you have some magic number of classes under your belt (and enough job experience), an amazing thing happens! You begin to realize that you didn't just learn the specifics of what each class taught you, you realize that along the way you picked up a big picture view of your job – where it fits in the scope of things at your company and in the industry. Now you're able to understand the benefits and ramifications of new technologies or products and how they can help or impact your company. This is when you start to become a really valuable contributor. You've become someone who has the ability to make strategic decisions on products, new product features and roadmaps.

Once you reach this enlightened stage of knowledge where you "get it" in regard to your job and its related technologies, you'll feel like you've arrived – that you have some legitimate skills which others don't. That's a good place to be, but it's not a good place to hang out for long. In other words, once you know something thoroughly there's a temptation to relax and stay in this comfort zone of what you've already learned and understand. However, technology is a fast moving target. You have to keep learning to stay current with the latest developments and innovations, or you risk dropping out of the leadership zone.

There will also be times during your career when you have to realize the technology area you've mastered isn't relevant anymore (i.e. a computer floppy disk designer). These are the hardest times to learn, because you have to mentally engage with the idea that you're not on top of things anymore and you're starting the learning process over again. However, the people who have job longevity are the ones who can reinvent themselves over and over again, learning brand new major technologies in the process.

The Five Year Plan

At any point in your professional life you should have "five year goals." Five years is out far enough that you're not constrained by having to think about your current job or the project that's currently consuming all your time and focus. You can dream a bit and think ideally about where you want to be. This is a good idea for your personal life as well. Too many people coast along, going with the flow and not having any personal goals. The question is whether you want to be the same exact person you are five years from now - or a new and improved version of yourself (i.e. a better job position or salary, being involved in healthy relationships and habits, making a difference in people's lives, etc.). It's a well established principle that the most successful people set inspiring goals for themselves. Unless you know where you're going, any road will do – and not all roads head in the right direction.

Five Years Gets Here Faster Than You Think (A.k.a. Time Flies When You're Having Fun)

On your way to the five year career milestone there will be logical times for you to evaluate where you're at and where you're headed (i.e. the end of one project and the start of another, transfer to a new group, restructuring, etc.). When these times occur, it's easy to take the path of least resistance and go wherever you're assigned (and that may be the right move). However, take those opportunities to evaluate whether there's something better. Maybe the group you're in has one of those PHB managers or you were hired in to a secondary group out of the main product loop. If there's an opportunity to transfer, go for it! Don't be like the moss or branch floating downstream, be like the salmon who knows they are going to an important destination, even if it's upstream. I realize this is not the best example since the salmon dies after getting there and doing their job, but you get the idea. 😃

Keep in mind that your second set of five year goals are often more important than your first – they should determine the long term shape of your career more than your first five year goal did. You've been on the job long enough now to see how different groups and people work together and get a sense of what your ideal job role would be during your prime career years (i.e. a senior technical role, management, sales, marketing, project management, etc.).

After I had been an engineer for the first five years of my career and burned through a couple of promotions to become a senior engineer, it was time to set a new five year goal. For me the decision was clear, I wanted to be in management. By this time, I had been through several projects and seen enough good and bad management decisions to have a pretty long mental library of situations I could have handled better. I grew to really dislike selfish and short-sighted management decisions that were more about protecting the manager's turf than for the good of the project or the company. I knew I could do a better job and I wanted the chance to try.

Another less than good situation I witnessed was engineers rise up through the ranks to get assigned management positions which they weren't prepared for and ended up not liking. They got promoted to a manager position because they were good engineers, but they were trying to manage people with the same skill set that made them a successful engineer - they didn't realize they had to develop a new skill set for the new role. Now don't get me wrong, not all the examples were bad. There were a few mid and high level managers doing a great job. Watching them confirmed my decision that I wanted to be like them - to have the influence and authority to make things (more) right in my corner of the company.

So I went out to develop a managerial skill set by getting an MBA. If I was going to do this management thing, I wanted to make sure I had the knowledge and skills to do a good job at it. By the way, I would recommend my approach to anyone who wants to get a master degree in anything. Get a job, start your career, get a clear idea of the career path you want and then go for the masters. Of course the best part of this approach is that your company pays for it! I realize this is not true in all cases, but whenever possible avoid personal debt for post-graduate education. This is the time in your career where you want to be saving some money for the marriage, kids, cars mortgages and such that are likely to be coming soon (which I proved you can do while paying for that first new car in your life :). I took my time getting the MBA, attending night classes after school, and a couple of weekend ones.

There were a couple of distractions that I took a term off for, like getting married and then a year later having our first child. But four years after starting (nine years into my career) I finally graduated and had my MBA. The timing was great too, because my wife was pregnant again and a couple of months after my graduation we had twins! There's no way I could have (or should have) gotten any school work done at home with two babies and a toddler in the house.

So how did my five year goal of becoming a manager turn out? The years before my graduation were busy ones. My company, Burroughs, had merged with Sperry and had become Unisys. There's always a couple years of corporate flux when something like that happens, when two nearly equal sized companies merge. Duplication of engineering effort had to be consolidated, product lines had to be merged and a new management culture started to emerge. On top of all that, my division had taken over development of a totally unique product invented by a genius PHD. It was an ASIC chip burn-in tester, the kind that people like Intel, AMD and Motorola now use to test their processors. It was great learning a new technology like this and all the intensely mechanical things that go with it (robotics, levers, pulleys, slide rails, hydraulics and such). But it was also disconcerting. As the project progressed my time was becoming nearly exclusively dedicated to it. The only ties I had back to the computer systems development group I had worked so closely with for the first 7+ years of my career were when a support problem came up that needed my attention. I felt like I had gotten out of a big caravan of cars headed down the freeway (with the big bosses and big money in the middle) and gotten off on a parallel side road that may or may not ever rejoin the big group on the main road. Yes, our group was very important and making a big profit at the time, but it worried me because it wasn't the core business of Unisys – computer systems.

So, a few months after graduating with my MBA, I found out there was a rare management opening back in the main computer systems development group. I ran as fast as I could to apply for it! I personally went to talk to the senior managers in that group to let them know I was applying, to stress my qualifications and enthusiasm for the job and how happy I was to have a chance to get back in the mainstream of what our company was doing. In reality, though, it wasn't an easy emotional decision. I had worked for the same director for seven years now, Dave. He was a manager with that rare combination of technical expertise, innovative vision and management savvy so that his decisions always made sense. He was my mentor (after Bill the Wookie) and I was extremely loyal to him. So I felt compelled to go to Dave and ask his blessing on my applying for this position. He was supportive, which I was really grateful for. However, even if he hadn't been, I'm 90% certain that my decision would have been the same – get the heck outta there. I remember wanting that job so bad I could taste it, and the delay between applying and hearing the management decision between me and the other candidates was grueling. It was one of the happiest days in my life when I was called in and told I got the job, just a couple of months after my ten year anniversary.

As a result of situations like this, one of the lessons I learned was patience. Setting important long term goals and working towards them takes a lot of patience. If the goals you set for yourself are something you can accomplish in a year, it's probably not a big enough goal.

Having a Work - Life Balance

At some point in your career, you will need to think about working less and enjoying your personal life more. You might be thinking, "Wait, what? What's this have to do with having a successful career"? Yes, there will be a time when you need to take these lessons and pack them into a normal 40-45 hour work week and scale back on the extra effort you put in to get your career started (at least from a time point of view). This is when you have to prioritize more and be smart about what things are fine to leave until tomorrow. Because being a successful person is more than just having a successful career. It's about having friends and family to share your successes with. It's about coming home to someone worth working for. It's about passing along the lessons you learned and making someone else better. It's about living a life of significance, not just success. To do this you need to invest the same kind of energy in your spouse or kids or family or friends that you do in your career. You want to leave a legacy in the hearts of those who love you, not just in the memories of those you worked with.

For me, this decision point came a year after I was married and our first child was born. I had to decide whether I wanted to be a constant presence every day in my kid's life, in tune with his first steps and the funny things he did and said, or whether I was going to be like Mr. Banks from Marry Poppins (come home from a day of being a successful businessman to pat the kid on the head and send him to bed with a hug and a kiss). Once I decided where my personal priority was (being a great dad) I had a scary decision to make. I had been the over the top achiever at work so long that I couldn't imagine scaling back. I was worried if I changed from the work pattern that made me successful that my job would be in danger at the very time I needed a steady income and benefits more than ever to take care of my family. Nevertheless, I went in on a

Monday morning with my priorities in order, ready for whatever consequences came along. When I explained the situation to my manager and that I was going to be working ~40 hours weeks to spend more time with my family, I got a stunning surprise. My boss said.... "Ok, no problem - I trust your judgment to get done what needs to be done". Wow! I had a hard time believing things would still be great and I would continue to learn and grow and progress. But you know what? I still got raises and promotions and new top tier project opportunities. Another lesson learned: a company will take all the hours you can give them in perpetuity but you can still succeed with a normal life and normal hours. Burning out is not good for you or them. I wouldn't trade those normal afternoon leaving times to coach baseball and soccer or to attend scout meetings for anything. Along the way I also discovered that the best things in life aren't things, they're the people you love and the time spent with them. And they are definitely something worth working hard for and being successful for. The pastor at my church said it this way, "Love people and use money. If you get those two reversed you'll never be happy."

More Stories

I'm glad that's over with.

One time we had a customer support trip to a small town in Texas. I was there with two other engineers, who kept a discussion going about how the place looked like an old time town from a 1950's western movie - complete with windblown sage brush tumbling through the town. It was so small that at breakfast the next morning at the Holiday Inn, the waitress said "Hey, ya'll are them boys workin' on the computers up at the hospital, aintcha?" After working late that night, the only place open late was a Pizza Hut. When we ordered the pizza, one of my fellow engineers - Andy, a big blustery funny Italian guy - wanted to order a beer with his pizza. The waitress said "I'm sorry sir, this is a dry county" (that means they don't sell any alcohol). "What?!" Andy yelled, pounding his fist on the table and scaring the waitress, "that's un-American, I never heard of such a thing!"

Working at the hospital had a weirdness factor as well. In one of the administrative rooms we had to install computer equipment in at the hospital, there were reminder tags on the terminals which said 'Run the deceased report on Monday mornings'... The whole place had a "Deliverance" (other-worldly) feel to it.

We finally got the job done and were on the way back to the DFW airport when one of those humongous torrential Texas downpours started - the kind where you can't see across the street. The windshield wipers couldn't keep up with the pace of the rain so we found ourselves inching along at 10 mph on the freeway using the 18 wheeler taillights 5 feet in front of us as a guide. We were concerned about someone running into us from behind, so Ken (the engineer in the back seat) said "I wonder if this car has airbags?" I pointed to Andy in the passenger seat and said "I know it at least has a passenger side one".

We were so glad to get out of there…

Another Andy story.

For a short while in his career, Andy tried being a manager. He didn't like it and went back to being an engineer, but during his short time as a manager I worked for him. One Monday Andy came over to my office and said "Phil, do you speak Spanish?" I told him I didn't but he said "you have to be in Guadalajara Mexico on Wednesday, see ya". He thought this was pretty funny until 16 long years later, when I was a manager and Andy worked for me. We had an important customer who needed support from our best engineer on that type of system. So I went over to Andy on a Monday morning and said "Andy, do you speak Korean?". He said no, then I said "you have to be in Seoul on Thursday, see ya" - at which point Andy yelled "Damn you! It took you 16 years but you finally got me back!" Of course he was laughing when he said it. Andy is retired now, but every time we get together we share a laugh about this story and many others.

Patience is a virtue, both at work and play.

One Saturday night my wife and I were on the way to the company's annual Christmas dinner/dance at a local hotel (ah, the good old days - we don't have those anymore in these tough economic times). We stopped at the bank ATM on the way so we would have some cash for the night. We had gotten a bit of a late start, so we were going to be there just on time barring any big delays. Of course the bank parking lot was packed, and on top of that a big SUV right in front of us stopped in the middle of the driveway (because there were no parking spots). They put on the flashers and it was clear they intended to park there while a man got out and walked to the ATM. My first impatient inclination was to lay on the horn and give those rude people what for, but I chilled and waited for a parking spot to open up behind them. When I got out to go to the ATM, boy was I glad I did! The man who got out of that SUV was walking back to his car now … and it was the corporate VP (my boss's boss)! I could have taken a major reputation and social hit if I had been impatient and laid on the horn.

Make the best of every situation with a good attitude.

I had been a manager about ten years, working for a company that was constantly shrinking and laying off engineers. During the last year or two of my managerial phase, we were laying off people once or twice a year. That wasn't fun at all. Like Forrest Gump, that's all I have to say about that. When the group of 22 that I managed was down to 5 and the manager of a peer group was down to 4, there was a management directive to combine the two groups into one. The director over his two line managers (us) had to make a decision as to who would be the remaining manager. The other manager was a great guy, but he had only been a manager for a couple of years and had a much smaller group before the layoffs. To me the decision was pretty clear about who should be the single manager over both groups combined into one. However, when the decision was made the director had chosen the other guy to be the manager!

At that point I had a choice. How was I going to handle this? Should I protest the decision and make a case for myself to be the manager? Would I accept the decision but harbor bitterness about it towards the new manager? Or would I see the change as a new opportunity and throw myself into the new technical non-managerial position and try to excel at it? Fortunately, I was able to man up and choose the latter option. It took a recommitment to one of my original career goals (be nice to everyone) but it turned out to be a great choice. About a year later, there was another big layoff in engineering. However, this one was specifically targeted at... managers. The new manager of the group was caught in the layoff and the few remaining engineers in our group worked directly for the previous manager's boss.

It's funny how things work out when you apply yourself fully to the job you're in without losing focus thinking about the job you're not in. Of course there's such a thing as developing the skills on your current job that will allow you to be promoted, that's a natural progression. Just be careful not to get to the point where you ever think your current job is below you or that you're entitled to a better position - there's a biblical principle that whoever is trustworthy with small things will be entrusted with bigger things. You can only do that if your heart is fully in the job you're in at the moment.

Ongoing Habits of Successful People

Current skills are relevant skills. One of the main things that every successful person keeps doing over and over (which is why I'm saying it over and over) – they never stop learning! When you get on the job you should be like a sponge, soaking up everything there is to know about your current job and your next job (what the required skills are to get a promotion to the next level). Once you have your arms around these enough to have some spare brain bandwidth, then go learn something new. Like how to use all the company infrastructure stuff that any senior engineer should know (how to pull a part number, how to get a part or document released, how to make hardware changes or software patches, etc.).

The more you know about how to do your job and all the periphery tasks associated with it, the more of an asset you will be to the company and your coworkers. Before you know it, you'll become a valuable asset to a various and assorted group of people who wouldn't want to imagine doing their job without you around. You will be someone who "makes this place better" (i.e. you make everyone around you better). So, if you are able to enjoy learning new things and seek them out you will rise up the list of valued employees. Plus you'll never be bored.

Successful people see problems as an opportunity where others see a problem as a problem. For example, in the 1995 movie Apollo 13 there was a point where just about everything that could go wrong with the spacecraft had. Part of it blew up and they had to try to limp home in a damaged landing module with maybe not enough fuel and not enough power to get back to earth, and on top of that they were running out of oxygen. Talk about a crisis! There's a scene where a NASA director is in the control room talking to a colleague, going over all the reasons why the trapped astronauts can't make it home. One of the directors says "I know what the problems are, this will be the worst disaster NASA has ever experienced". Ed Harris's character (flight director Gene Kranz) overhears their conversation and replies, "with all due respect sir, I believe this is going to be our finest hour". And it was! Gene's team worked around the clock and came up with some innovative solutions that ended up saving the spacecraft and the astronauts. Now that's a person that knew how to rally in the face of adversity!

Will you be able to have that attitude when your customer's computer system is down and they need it up by 6:00am in the morning or else revenue is lost or planes can't take off? When a potential customer's pending purchase decision on a new solution is dependent on a feature your team can't get working in the lab? When your project is behind schedule and manager's start implementing the blame game policy? You get the idea. Your ability to rise above the frustration of the situation and have a great attitude will your opportunity – to shine, to motivate others, to lead, to be a "Gene". You can't control everything that happens to you, but you can control your reaction to it.

Successful people make their boss happy. Not a brown-noser schmoozer or Yes-man kind of happy. But the "I'm going to do a great job for you, so you and our team look good" kind of happy. There are two general camps employees fall into. One kind needs daily direction on what the priorities and tasks are. The other can take a goal and run with it – go off and talk to people to learn how to do that job and only come back to the manager for big "I'm stuck" or course correction questions. Both can be great employees, but if you want to be a leader you'll develop the work habits it takes to be in the latter group. Those are the kind of people bosses trust and give more responsibility to. You'll know you're getting to this level of trust and responsibility when the boss is going to be gone and asks you to sit in for him or her at meetings.

More on the topic of keeping your boss happy

Keeping your management informed of problems is absolutely necessary, but don't go to your boss with a problem which you haven't first thought about how to solve. You should be able to present solution options at the same time as the problem, or at least what the next steps are to work towards a solution. In most cases, your next step would be a plan to diagnose the problem's root cause. So you would communicate the problem and its scope (who it affects and the consequences) and then the going forward plan, including the resources and estimated time needed to diagnose the cause. If the problem is unique enough so that it's hard to estimate the time and resources needed, present the plan as an initial outlook or plan in progress. The only wrong answer is to have no plan. Going in without a plan is like saying you can't handle it and you want them to fix it for you.

Speaking of plans, planning is another thing successful people do. You might have heard the expression "People who fail to plan … plan to fail." You should get in the habit of spending a few minutes each morning thinking about what you have to do that day and prioritizing what to do first. There will be some things which are the most important and must get done while others could wait until tomorrow or next week. The way that works best for me is to always have an action list – a notebook with handwritten notes or a computer file that lists every open action I have regardless of the due date. Once you can see everything all at once it's much easier to prioritize actions and plan your activity. Plus you'll be a lot less likely to ever have open actions drop off your radar without addressing them.

Successful people are good communicators. Learn to communicate and you will be able to communicate to learn. When you're actually interested in what someone has to say instead of thinking about your reply and how urgent it is for the other person to hear what you have to say – you will be a good listener and learn a lot! Put yourself in their shoes for a minute and all kinds of questions come up that will help you understand instead of just hearing. For example, if you meet a person at your company whose job is product documentation your question might be how much they need to know about the products they are documenting. Do they have to get a demo from engineering and learn the product well enough to use and understand it, or do they just take documentation provided by engineers and publish it in the right format? You can learn from anyone who has a job at your company.

There are a lot of people involved with designing, delivering, selling and supporting technology products. Asking questions and really listening to people's stories will help you get your arms around the whole company or industry concept and where your job fits in the big picture. You will need this perspective for any senior leadership role.

Successful people accept criticism without getting defensive. Even when criticism is intended to be derogatory, answering with something like "Thanks, I'll go think about that" immediately puts a wet blanket on the fire of any argument that's about to start. If the criticism is intended to be constructive, you can nearly always learn something from it. Go away and think about what they said (after the emotion of the moment subsides) then sift through it to see if there are any truths you want to pull out. They could have a point! Nobody is right all the time and we aren't always going to be told so through gentle encouragement.

Successful people have the confidence and initiative to think outside the box and try things that haven't been done before. For example, after my transition from the management position back to a technical one, I found myself working for a director in another location (back east). I had a sense of social vertigo that came from being the only west coast member of the team and not having any local management. I guess some people would view this as a welcome freedom from daily supervision, but in my experience the more out of touch with management you are the more expendable you become.

On one occasion, I learned that my boss's boss would be travelling out west to Silicon Valley. This big boss was someone I had met a couple of times over the years but didn't have a close relationship with - which wasn't a good thing since he was the head of engineering and the technical expert behind many of the major product and staffing decisions that got made. He would be in San Jose to get a presentation on a company's technology and how it fit for possible integration with our products. This kind of technology was something I understood and had actually evaluation tested similar products in the engineering lab. So I got the bright idea to volunteer myself to go there and help. I told my boss that I would pay my own way to go and would do it on a vacation day if necessary (this wasn't a huge financial commitment, since where I worked in Orange County was an hour long $98 flight away – for a grand total of $147 with the rental car and lunch). There weren't any grounds for objection, since I was paying, so off I went.
The meeting went very well. I got a chance to drive most of the technical discussion and take the lead on post-meeting follow up actions with this company. It was the first time I got to spend more than five minutes with the big boss and actually work with him. It got our relationship started and going to the point where a year or so later I was asked to work on a three person Cloud technology team with him! I'm not sure this opportunity would have come along if I hadn't done something out of the box to jump start the relationship.

Random Strategic Advice

Back to the topic of professionalism and protecting your reputation. Once you're into your career, avoid drastic changes in your looks (wardrobe, hair, grooming, visible piercings or tattoos, etc.). Big changes like this are viewed as instability and a lack of confidence in who you are. Your management might not call you on the carpet over it, but it will be a topic in their discussion when you're up for a promotion, raise or bonus. If you were a customer of your company dealing with your team, would you feel confident dealing with someone who suddenly changed their looks and appears like they are going through some kind of life or identity crisis? You might think that this person has a lot going on and might not care if they drop the ball on your account. You owe it to your company to look professional. A corollary to this rule is to never show up to a company event under-dressed (i.e. jeans when everyone else is business casual, or business casual at a formal meeting where everyone is wearing a tie). You can always take off a tie or jacket but you can't conjure up better clothes on a moment's notice. Showing up for important events unprepared (under-dressed) shows everyone the situation is not important to you.

Don't let your career be tripped up by events going on in your personal life (i.e. relationship problems). At some point during your career you could have challenges due to arguments, money problems, car problems, divorce, medical issues, teenager problems, etc. - sometimes nearly all of them at once! You don't want to add your job to the list of things in a crisis situation. The people that let their work suffer during these situations are usually the ones that spend all their emotional energy on things they can't control.

When you're at work, give it a rest and try to concentrate fully on your job. You'll find that doing a good job at work is therapeutic and can help you put your problems in a healthier perspective.

Be generous with your praise and give credit when it's due. Praise is something that you should give whenever you see someone going above and beyond their normal job duties or even excelling in their normal tasks. It's energizing to the person you praise and it validates their work ethic - people deserve to be appreciated for making decisions that help the team and their company to succeed. Not only that, but when you can become a habitual praise giver and encourager, pretty soon you'll find people going out of their way to help you and encourage you as well. Team building 101 – look for genuine opportunities to praise. By genuine I mean something actually worthy of being praised. You're praise will start to lose its value if you waste it on an average effort or even a successful job that didn't require much effort. Make them earn it, but be generous with your praise when they do.

Sharing credit for a successful team effort is essential, even if you are the team leader or the primary contributor. By doing this you're acknowledging that you work for a company whose success is important to you, and that it's not "all about me." You're also building a reputation as a team player instead of a narcissist who has to get recognition for every accomplishment. There is a time to blow your own horn – at a year-end discussion with your manager in a performance review or on a resume. But not in daily work at the expense of your coworkers. People want to work with and for someone who can share the credit for a job well done.

Yet More Stories

Believe it or not, practical jokes can build camaraderie in a team. As long as the pranks are harmless and don't waste more than a few minutes of company time, the humor they provide can be a big stress reliever.

One time, on April Fool's day, our team was in the middle of a project working on three large mainframe computers. The keyboards on these systems were programmable, so I got the bright idea to have some April Fool's day fun and lighten the group up in the process. I went in before normal starting time and programmed the space bars of the keyboards on all three systems to reboot the machines! I stood back and watched the fun when the engineers arrived to start the shift. When the first reboot happened there was some confusion, like what the heck just happened? After the second one, the engineers were tentatively pecking each key on the keyboard until they hit the space bar and then boom! another reboot. By this time frustration was building and probably would have continued into a meltdown except that I couldn't stop laughing. After they figured out what had happened we all had a good laugh about it and the work that day seemed more light-hearted and productive than it had been in days.

Another time we had a visit from a very senior engineer from the east coast, who helped us with a particular part of our project. The guy was professional and got his job done, but he was edgy and angry to the point where people were walking on eggshells around him - afraid to say something that would cause another harsh snapping response.

Just before quitting time one day, me and another engineer noticed his briefcase open in the engineering lab. We looked at each other with a "Fred and George Weasley gleam" in our eyes and knew what had to be done. We took a bunch of the plastic packing peanuts from a box we received that day and stuffed them in his briefcase and sat on it to get it shut and locked. Sure enough, when the snooty engineer got back to the lab he picked up his briefcase and headed to the exit not noticing that he had left it open and it was now closed. These were the days in which our company had tightened security so that everyone's briefcase or backpack had to be checked by the guard on the way out, so we followed him and hoped that hilarity would ensue. We were not disappointed. The engineer set his briefcase down on the guard's counter and turned it so the guard could open it. Once the locks were released, boom! all of the plastic pieces went up in the air and covered the guard's area - including some resting on the top of the guard's hat! The guard gave the engineer a look that could have curdled milk but all he could do was sputter something about "I didn't do this, really, I don't know!" After he helped clean up the mess (there wasn't that much) he took off and we didn't see him until the next day. It's funny, he seemed to have a new attitude and wasn't as hard to get along with any more. I think he realized that someone had 'poked him in the ribs' for his annoying attitude and he cleaned it up.

Your career is like driving a car
(isn't everything?)

Your technical skills are the car. How good you are at developing critical job skills will determine whether you're cruising along in a deep-breathing muscle car with plenty of headroom to accelerate or whether you're pedal to the metal in a rust bucket with a bunch of screaming hamsters under the hood struggling to keep up with the flow of traffic.

Your integrity and professionalism are the quality of the parts the car is built with and how the car was constructed from the parts. Will you have what it takes to go through the perilous road conditions of a challenging job? Or will you break down when the going gets tough?

Your goals, ambition and work ethic are the fuel that will allow the car to go a long distance (lots of fuel) or a short distance (not so much). Will you be someone who needs tune-ups (from management) all the time, doing just enough to satisfy the job requirements? Or will you be a proactive do-everything-right achiever who has an unlimited supply of gas in the tank?

Your reputation will determine what roads are open for you to drive on. Without a good reputation you'll find yourself looking at your destination (career goals) and realizing you can't get there from here. The better your reputation is the more roads (opportunities) open up for you.

Your relationships will determine whether you are driving the car of your car-eer or if you're just a passenger along for the ride going to a destination that someone else happens to be headed for. Your relationships will also determine how much help you have along the way. When you have to change a flat tire or its time for a tune-up or you need a little body work from a fender bender, will you being trying to go it alone or will you have someone working with you - someone whose got your back.

Wrapping It Up

Getting started on a new job, especially your first one, is an exciting time! You have clean slate for building a great reputation and the opportunity to establish new relationships. Your ability to do these things well will determine whether you make it to the decision making group or stay in the decision taking group. I hope you will use the negative don't-do-this examples in this book to avoid at least a few of the mistakes I made, or saw made. Even better, I hope you will be inspired by the positive examples to do things that will lead to great successes for you.

I recommend that you save this book in your library as a reference book. Go back to take a look at it once in a while. Since I covered various situations that could come up in the first ten years or so of your career, not all of the advice will be meaningful at a certain point in time, but it will eventually.

Here is a handy reminder of things to do and not to do, in the form of ATTA boys or ATTA girls (Actions To Think About).

Do's

Set high standards for yourself
Understand your Reputation and Relationships
Complete professionalism
Communicate well
Evaluate your progress
Stay the course
Stop whining!

SUCCESS

Set high standards for yourself – This is doing every job well and refusing to fail no matter what problems come up along the way. When you succeed with the jobs you're assigned, you'll get greater responsibility and greater career opportunities.

Understand your reputation and relationships are critically important to your success. Treat them with care!

Complete professionalism – Accept nothing less. Never let any task, project or e-mail conversation end without proper closure. Meet every commitment you make, even if it involves significant personal sacrifice.

Communicate well – If you don't, you won't learn what you need to know and you won't be able to teach others effectively - bottom line, you won't become a leader.

Evaluate your progress – Set goals that are worth achieving, plan how to make them happen and then get moving! If changes at work put you in a place that isn't going to help achieve these goals long term, look for opportunities to move up or over. You have more options than you think.

Stay the course - There will be days or weeks when your job sucks and you don't feel like going to work. This is normal with any job! Don't make an emotional decision to change careers or jobs during these times that will soon pass.

Stop whining! – You have a degree and will have a job soon. You know where your next meal is coming from and you have a home and probably a car – you're already in the top 5% of wealthy people in the world! Be grateful for what you have and don't take it for granted. You are blessed to have what you have and be gainfully employed. Don't have a pity party when things get bad, they could be a lot worse. There are hard-working blue collar people who have never had an opportunity for higher education, who ride a bus an hour each way to a menial labor job that pays a fraction of what you will be making.

Don't

Forget to keep your word
Allow compromise
Involve yourself in toxic relationships
Lose opportunities to learn

FAIL

DON'T...

Forget to keep your word – The easiest way to fail is to be someone who can't be counted on. With a lack of trust comes a lack of value to your coworkers and the company.

Allow compromise – Always do business with integrity. If you allow small compromises in your business habits and character (i.e. lying on schedules, expense reports, etc.) bigger ones will follow.

Involve yourself in toxic relationships - Of course you can help people out who are headed in the wrong direction. Inspire, encourage and teach them – pull them up. But your primary close relationships should be with people that make you better – people that pull you up.

Lose opportunities to learn – Get a mentor! You will be better for the experience and so will they. Then when you are ready, be one for someone else. You don't fully understand something until you have to explain it to someone. That process will expose any gaps in your knowledge, which you can then work on correcting.

A Call to Action

So there you have it, my take on how to have a successful career. A great career is produced by great character, attitude and work ethic. When you have these three things in order, by investing in and protecting your reputation and relationships, you can’t go wrong. Problems may come and go, but you won’t.

The start of your career is an opportunity to become the person you want to be known as professionally. Seize the day! Get out there and make some great accomplishments and memories. These are your good ole days…

Bibliography

http://en.wikipedia.org/wiki/Six_phases_of_a_big_project

The cynical version of:

Six Phases of a Project

1. Enthusiasm
2. Disillusionment
3. Panic
4. Search for the guilty
5. Punishment of the innocent
6. Praise and honors for the non-participants

Thanks

I want to thank the following significant people in my career, who helped write this book by providing me with invaluable career lessons and examples along the way.

Mom and Dad, Dave M. the wise, Sheila, Kelly (I miss you man), Agnes, Chris W., Ron the professional, big Bill S., Michelle, big boss Bill T., Chuckie, Ken the joker, Jeff, boo-boo Bob, Greg G. a man of integrity, Wes, Arif, Giri, Ralph, Elizabeth, Mike I., Sam, Cal, Herman, Jim T., Jim J., Jake the crazy Israeli, Guy, Alan and Julie, Dorothy, Gibson, David S., Jean, Dick, Serena, Will, Tom L., Ed, Mike R. the best employee ever ("it's always Mike's fault!"), Wieki, Chris C., Kevin the best employee ever (tie), Greg S., Chris the genius programmer dude, Wayne the technical genius, Darryl the over-achiever, Mike A., Norm ("do good and fight evil"), Jane, Susan, John G., Jose, Don T. (DrT my best buddy), Steve H., Dan W., Don L., Andy (thanks man), Dennis W., Ken H., Craig, Sue, Lee, Tom L, Ed, George the super nice Scotty, Dr. Scott, David C., Tick-Tock Tony, Pastor Rick, Tim and Darci, Richard, James the geek (you rock!), Dennis C., Lee, Diana the encourager, Lynn, Tom S. ("It doesn't get any better than this"), David F., John H., Ray, Mark the ultimate professional, Steve G. my mentor, Penny (PLS II), Al, Chris the great GM, Gord, Ness, Dave R., Larry, Diep, and Tom T. the super star.

Made in the USA
Monee, IL
04 November 2026

67380500R10036